LOUIS PASTEUR

Richard Tames

Franklin Watts

New York • London • Sydney • Toronto

Contents

© 1990 Franklin Watts

Franklin Watts Inc.
387 Park Avenue South
New York, N.Y. 10016

Phototypeset by: JB Type, Hove, East Sussex
Printed in: Belgium
Series Editor: Hazel Poole
Editor: Dee Turner
Designed by: Nick Cannan

Tames, Richard.
    Louis Pasteur / Richard Tames.
      p.   cm. — (Lifetimes)
    Includes bibliographical references.
    Summary: Follows the life story of Louis Pasteur, from his modest
beginnings to his study of chemistry and his discovery of cures for
such infectious diseases as rabies and anthrax.
    ISBN 0-531-14025-3
    1. Pasteur, Louis, 1822-1895—Juvenile literature. 2. Scientists—
France—Biography—Juvenile literature. 3. Chemists—France—
Biography—Juvenile literature. 4. Microbiologists—France—
Biography—Juvenile literature. [1. Pasteur, Louis. 1822-1895.
2. Scientists.] I. Title. II. Series: Lifetimes (London, England)
Q143.P2T36 1990
509.2—dc20
[B]
[92]   89-29278
                                     CIP AC

The Tanner's Son

Louis Pasteur was one of the greatest scientists — perhaps *the* greatest — of the nineteenth century. Yet he was born, on December 27, 1822, into a simple peasant family in Dôle, a small town near the mountains of eastern France. As a boy he showed more talent for painting than for science, but once he had become fascinated by chemistry he devoted his hardworking life to this subject. By the time of his death, his discoveries had made him revered by millions of people who knew nothing about science, for he had made possible the conquering of so many forms of suffering and disease, including the

Pasteur's birthplace in Dôle (above). **His father** (left) **was a well-respected tradesman.**

deadly diseases of anthrax and rabies. Even his name entered the language as a scientific word — **pasteurization**.

Louis' father, Jean-Joseph, was a tanner, treating animal skins to turn them into leather that could be used to make saddles and other useful items. He was following in a family tradition, for members of the Pasteur family had been in the

The family tannery made Pasteur aware of industry, while brilliant Dumas (below) **inspired him to study.**

tanning business for generations. No doubt this experience as a boy started Louis' lifelong interest in the practical problems of industry and commerce, and the part that science could play in overcoming them. Jean-Joseph had also been a sergeant major in Napoleon's army, and from him Louis inherited a strong love of his country. His parents were ambitious for him, but their greatest ambition was that he should become a teacher in a local school. They could hardly guess that he would become a world-famous scientist.

Pasteur's early education took place in Arbois, a small town in the hills where his family had moved to live. He soon showed a talent for art, and became very good at painting portraits. In an effort to push forward his academic career, his father sent Louis away to school in Paris when he was sixteen. But after a month, young Louis was so homesick that his parents let him come home again. After studying as far as he could at college in Besançon, he did at last return to Paris, where he attended a private school and a **lycée**, before finally entering the prestigious École Normale Supérieure. The inspired teaching of the chemist J.B. Dumas, whose lectures Louis Pasteur attended at the **Sorbonne**, set his life on a new course. Fascinated and excited by the study of chemistry, he soon began to undertake research of his own.

Pasteur's first work was in the field of **crystallography**. Many chemical substances can be made to

produce crystals, which are solids that have a regular, geometric shape. Observation of these crystals and the way they react under different conditions can provide interesting information about the substances which produce them. Pasteur tested the ways in which light was affected when it shone on crystals of tartaric acid, an acid formed when grapes are fermented to make wine. He used these observations to show how the structure of tartaric acid differed from racemic acid, a substance not previously understood, that was made up of the same chemical elements as tartaric acid but behaved differently. As a result of these researches, Pasteur later came to be recognized as the founder of what is known as **stereochemistry**.

This research also brought him instant fame at the age of 26, and marked him out for a brilliant career. He was made a member of the Legion of Honor by the French government. The Royal Society in England sent him a special gold medal. He was briefly given a job as a schoolteacher, but the Ministry of Education allowed him special leave so that he could go on with his research work. Soon he was promoted to Professor of Chemistry at the University of Strasbourg, where he met and married Marie Laurent, the daughter of the head of the university. They were to have

five children, but only two of them survived beyond childhood.

Throughout his life, whether teaching or researching, Pasteur put in long hours, working into the night and often through Sundays as well. He had an immense power of concentration and great stamina and, once he focused on a problem, was unwilling to let it go until he had solved it. When he died he left behind over 100 notebooks full of details of his experiments. He recognized the part played by chance in making new discoveries, but never believed that great advances were simply the result of accident. Chance, he was fond of saying, only favors the mind that is already prepared.

Pasteur the Painter

As a young boy, Pasteur showed remarkable talent as an artist, making pastel portraits of his parents, teachers, friends and classmates. Even the mayor of his home town, Arbois, and other local officials came to pose for him. The headmaster of his college in Besançon displayed one of Pasteur's portraits in the entrance hall for everyone to admire. Pasteur, however, was unmoved by the praise he received and assured his parents in a letter home that academic honors were more important to him, saying:

"I would rather be first in college than receive 10,000 compliments … "

Pasteur was as good as his word and gave up taking art lessons so that he could concentrate on his studies. But he continued to paint during his days off — always portraits, never landscapes or any other subject. However, he did go on to use his artistic talents in the course of his scientific career. When giving lectures he could illustrate what he was saying with clear, well-drawn pictures. And from 1863 to 1867 he taught special courses at the École des Beaux-Arts in Paris, showing how science could be applied to art and architecture. From his lectures, students learned the chemistry of paints and colors, how to make porcelain or enamel, and how to design buildings that were well ventilated, as well as beautiful.

A French art critic once commented that Pasteur, if he had not become a scientist, could have been "a good painter, maybe one of the greatest."

The Pasteur family home in Arbois is now preserved as a museum in honor of France's most famous scientist.

Savior of Industry

In 1854, Pasteur was made head of the science department at the new University of Lille, an industrial city where the making of wine and beer were major sources of local wealth and employment. Pasteur responded to his new situation with energy and imagination. Because he believed that science should have practical uses, and that university teachers and businessmen should not live in two separate worlds, he began to organize evening classes for working men and to take his students on visits to factories. Encouraged by his down-to-earth approach to learning, a local industrialist asked Pasteur to help him out with a problem. The man's business was to produce vinegar from **beet** juice. Sometimes the **fermentation** process seemed to go wrong and the result was a spoiled product that could only be thrown away. Similar problems also happened very often in the manufacture of wine and beer, causing millions of dollars to be wasted in time and materials.

Pasteur carefully collected samples of fermenting juices and examined them systematically under a microscope. He soon found that when wine and beer age properly, the liquid contained tiny yeast cells that were round in shape. When the process went wrong, however, the

wine or beer turned sour and the yeast cells were long and narrow, not round. He concluded that there were two types of yeast — a useful one that would produce alcohol, and a damaging one that would produce lactic acid. Even more important, from the point of view of chemical theory, he showed that fermentation involves living organisms and is not simply a chemical process. **Microorganisms**, tiny living forms visible only under a microscope, were in fact the cause.

Realizing it was the lactic acid that damaged the fermenting wine, Pasteur looked for a practical solution to the problem. He found a simple answer — heating the wine gently to about 140°F (60°C) killed off any harmful yeast. The winemakers were horrified at the idea of heating wine and were sure that it would spoil the taste. To

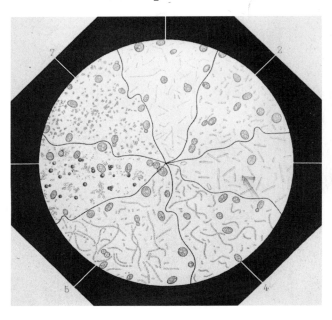

An illustration from Pasteur's book on beer shows a microscope view of fermenting organisms.

convince them, Pasteur put his theory to a straightforward public test and divided a batch of wine into two. One was heated and the other left unheated. Months later, all the heated samples were found to be fine and their flavor perfect. Several samples from the unheated batch had gone sour. The process of gentle heating to kill off unwanted microorganisms was quickly applied to other stored liquids, especially milk, and was soon known as "pasteurization" in honor of its inventor. The process is, of course, widely used today and has helped to make our food and drink safe.

Pasteur stayed only three years in Lille. In 1857, though only 35 years of age, he was appointed Director of Studies at the École Normale Supérieure, back in Paris. It was an

This simple pan (above) was used by Pasteur in his wine-heating experiments. The picture below shows a German milk pasteurizer based on the principles he discovered.

important appointment for so young a man, but it carried with it no facilities for research, no laboratory or grant to pay for assistants or equipment. Pasteur paid for these himself and equipped a laboratory at his own expense in two tiny attic rooms at the college. They were so small and cramped that he had to enter them on his knees. But the work he did there helped to ensure his continued promotion. In 1862 he was elected to the Academy of Sciences and in 1863 began to teach his new "science for artists" course at the École des Beaux-Arts, as well.

His interest in yeast cells led him on from the process of fermentation to the question of how microscopic life-forms arose in the first place. At that time, scientists were divided on the matter. Some believed in the

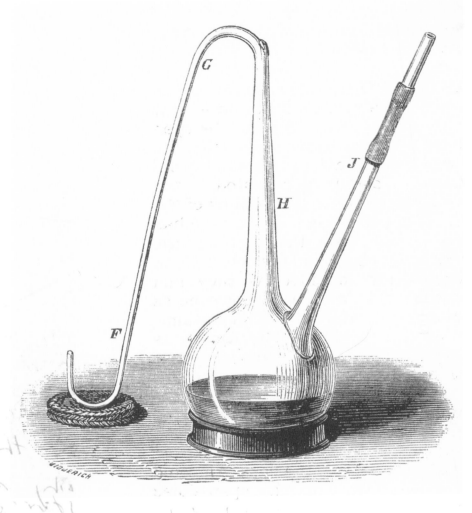

This "swan-neck" flask was used by Pasteur to show that putrefaction was caused by airborne organisms and not by "spontaneous generation."

theory of spontaneous generation — the belief that such tiny beings simply arose out of dead matter, without any living "parents," as it were. Others believed this was impossible and looked for some other cause, but they were not quite sure what it might be. Pasteur felt strongly that the second view was right. He set out to prove that living things could not arise spontaneously out of dead matter, but must be the product of some other form of life. The offer of a prize to settle the matter one way or the other gave Pasteur the final incentive to devise a series of experiments to prove his point.

By breathing through a fine cotton mask, Pasteur showed that it was possible to filter out the spores of living organisms that are carried by the dust in the ordinary air we breathe. He believed that it was these spores, rather than the action of the air as such, that gave birth to new organisms as living matter decayed. He then tested his theory by putting samples of test materials in flasks. Some were sealed up after

Pasteur in the Jura mountains — a spectacular example of his concern for practical experiment.

the air in them had been heated to kill off the spores. Others were left open. The test material in the open flasks went bad and spawned microorganisms; the sealed ones did not. Pasteur repeated the experiment in the mountains of the Jura, the region near where he had been born. At the foot of the mountains he found that material in open flasks decayed as they had done in the Paris tests. However, as he went higher up the mountains, the contents of fewer of the flasks started to decay — because the thinner air contained fewer spores.

Another neat illustration of the process devised by Pasteur involved the use of a flask with a long V-shaped neck. Boiled meat extract was placed inside the flask. Air could get to it through the open-ended neck, but dust (containing microorganisms) was trapped at the curve of the V. No decay took place; no organisms developed in the boiled meat extract. In 1862, Pasteur was awarded the prize for finding out about microorganisms. In 1864 a committee of scientists, including Pasteur's old teacher, Dumas, studied the results of all Pasteur's experiments and found the case against spontaneous germination decisively proved. Invisible, and before now unknown, living cells in the air had been shown to exist.

Joseph Lister

Lister (1827–1912) was a brilliant English surgeon who recognized that researchers often found solutions to practical problems. The introduction of effective **anesthetics** in the 1840s increased the number of surgical operations that could be performed, because far fewer patients died of shock. However, the new problem was that so many patients now died from infections contracted during the operation and recovery period.

In 1865, Lister read about Pasteur's work on fermentation and his belief that decaying was caused by living organisms. Lister realized that lives could be saved if these infecting organisms could be destroyed. So he began using carbolic acid to clean surgical wounds and to keep dressings sterile. At once, death rates among his patients began to fall. This was the beginning of **antiseptics**, which have since saved so many lives.

Lister wrote to Pasteur:

"If you ever come to Edinburgh, I think it would be a real reward to you to see in our hospital how immensely humankind has profited by your work."

It took a long time for other surgeons to realize that Lister was right, but by the end of his long life he was recognized and honored as a great innovator who had enormously lessened the suffering of hospital patients.

Lister, aged about 40. Unlike Pasteur, he had to battle for the recognition that his methods were scientifically based.

The Miracle Man

Pasteur was by now the miracle man of France. When a disastrous disease broke out in 1865, killing off silkworms and threatening the valuable silk industry of southern France, the government pleaded with Pasteur to find a remedy. For once, he was hesitant and asked his old teacher Dumas for advice. "I have never worked with silkworms," Pasteur pointed out. "So much the better," retorted Dumas, arguing that he would bring a fresh mind to the problem.

Pasteur traveled to the south of France with his microscope and set up a makeshift laboratory. Within four months he had identified the tiny parasite that was infesting the silkworms and the mulberry leaves they fed on. After three years he came to the conclusion that only the most drastic action could save the industry. All infested worms and mulberry bushes would have to be destroyed and a new start made with fresh, healthy silkworms. Pasteur's reputation was so high that this tough advice was accepted. He also showed farmers how to avoid the illness in the silkworms recurring, and the industry was saved.

By this time, his dedication to research and a series of family tragedies combined to make him give up much of his teaching and administration. In 1865 his father died; his two-year-old daughter, Camille, died soon after. The following year, his 12-year-old daughter, Cécille, was killed by typhoid fever. In 1867 he stopped teaching at the École des Beaux-Arts and stepped down as Director of Scientific Studies at the École Normale. Thanks to the direct support of Emperor Napoleon III, a special research laboratory was created for him. But, although this left him free to concentrate on his own work, it did nothing to stop him from working too hard. In 1868, when he was 46, he suffered a stroke which permanently paralyzed part of his left arm and his left leg. For the rest of his career as an experimental scientist, he had to rely on assistants to perform all but the simplest laboratory work.

Making silk circa 1855. Pasteur saved this major French industry from almost certain collapse.

France's defeat by **Prussia** in the Franco-Prussian War of 1870–71 had a profound effect on Pasteur; but he also had a profound effect on the soldiers who fought in that war. He tried to volunteer for active service, though still partly paralyzed, and was gently told to return to his microscope. The only gesture of defiance he could make towards his country's enemy was to return an honorary degree awarded to him by the University of Bonn and icily request that his name be removed from its records. As a Frenchman he was deeply distressed by his country's humiliation and loss

Pasteur benefited from the interest of Napoleon III (left), whose downfall came with the Franco-Prussian war.

of the territory of Alsace-Lorraine. But as a scientist he saw that the suffering wounded could benefit immensely if only the army medical teams would accept his theories. If they accepted that infection was caused by microbes, they could greatly limit human suffering by sterilizing surgical instruments and bandages. Because he was Pasteur, the army doctors listened. And the results were spectacular. As a result, in 1873 he was elected a member of the French Academy of Medicine — a remarkable tribute to a man without formal qualifications as a doctor.

Pasteur was still, of course, regarded by wine- and beer-makers as the great authority on the application of science to their industries, and they accepted his published studies on wine (1866) vinegar (1868) and beer (1876) as standard works. It was even said that his discoveries had saved these industries more money than was being claimed by Germany after France's defeat. Certainly, Pasteur himself hoped that, by helping the French brewing industry to become more efficient, he could assist it in beating back the tide of imported beer from Germany. He even patented a new method of brewing beer and hoped to market it under the label "Beer of the National Revenge." Ironically, he never drank beer himself. Even wine he drank sparingly. But he was altogether rather fanatical about cleanliness, as a man obsessed with **germs** might be expected to be. He even thought the English custom of shaking hands was rather unhealthy!

Edward Jenner

(Far left) **A French artist's idea of what it might have been like when Jenner** (left) **began to experiment with cowpox vaccination.**

Edward Jenner (1749–1823) was an English country doctor who helped lay the foundation of **immunization**. He noticed that milkmaids almost never suffered from that disfiguring scourge of the eighteenth century — smallpox. Investigation led him to believe that they had become **immune** to the illness as a result of contracting cowpox, a related but much milder disease. Jenner began to infect patients with cowpox deliberately, to make them immune from the deadlier threat of smallpox. The idea worked. Despite this success, Jenner was content to live in obscurity and remained a country doctor all his life.

Pasteur readily acknowledged Jenner as the inspiration for his own work in developing **vaccines** to combat anthrax, rabies and other infectious diseases.

The Relief of Suffering

Pasteur's next great field of investigation was the way in which diseases were spread among humans and animals. He focused first of all on anthrax, a deadly killer of domestic animals that every year destroyed one sheep in five in France. Some doctors denied that any germs (microorganisms) at all were involved in this disease, but Pasteur's great German rival, Robert Koch, claimed in 1876 to have detected the germs responsible. Pasteur ran his own tests and not only confirmed Koch's findings, but showed that these germs could survive for long periods in the ground. In other words, an infected herd could pollute the field in which it grazed, passing the sickness on to a healthy herd using the same field at a later date.

Pasteur's initial solution was the same as in the case of silkworm disease — kill the infected animals, burn their bodies and bury the remains deep underground to cut off the chance of reinfection. Then he thought again. If an animal did survive an attack of anthrax, it

A Paris magazine illustrates the inoculation of sheep against anthrax in 1882.

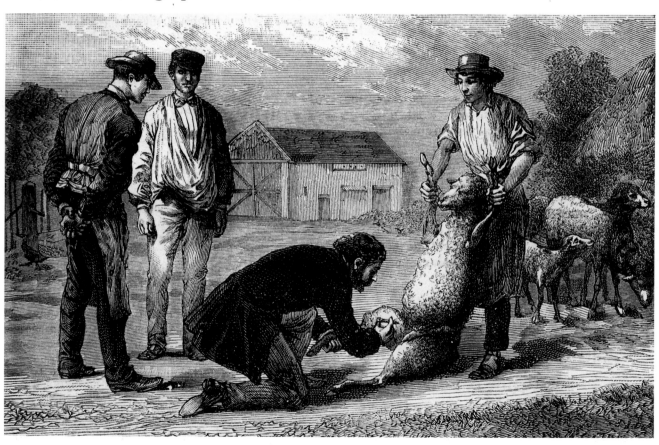

became immune to any further attack. Almost a century earlier, Edward Jenner had shown how to ward off smallpox by **inoculation**, that is, giving people cowpox deliberately. This mild version of the disease made them immune to smallpox itself. There was no naturally mild version of anthrax, so Pasteur made his own by heating up a preparation of anthrax germs to weaken them. In 1881 he carried out a dramatic experiment, similar to the heated wine demonstration of a quarter of a century before. This time he divided a flock of 50 sheep into two equal groups, one of which was inoculated with the weakened anthrax germs. Some time later the whole flock was inoculated with full-strength anthrax germs. The group that had been previously inoculated with weakened anthrax proved to be entirely immune to anthrax. The others all died.

Similar methods were used to combat chicken cholera, which was killing ten percent of all the fowl in France every year, and swine fever, which in 1878 had killed 1 million pigs in the United States.

Pasteur's discoveries saved farmers and manufacturers vast amounts of money and so were of great economic benefit to France. The French government recognized this by giving him control of about ten percent of all its yearly spending on science. It also gave him a personal payment of 25,000 francs a year so that he would have no financial anxieties and would be free to concentrate on his research work. Science not only made Pasteur famous; it made him rich as well.

But wealth did not stop him working as hard as ever. A letter from his wife to his daughter paints the picture briefly and accurately:

"Your father, very busy as always, says little to me, sleeps little, and gets up at dawn — in a word, continues the life that I began with him 35 years ago today."

Now over 60 years old, crippled and in failing health, Pasteur faced his most testing challenge — rabies. It was the ultimate killer disease and its victims died slowly, horribly and in great agony. But Pasteur reasoned that if he could produce a weakened form of the rabies virus, he might be able to use it as a protective vaccine. At grave risk to himself, he used glass tubes to suck saliva from the foaming mouths of rabid dogs, then injected it into rabbits. When the disease took hold in the rabbits he extracted their spinal cords and dried them out, hoping that this would weaken the virus with which they were infected. He then made an extract from cords which had dried out over a period of fourteen days. When this was injected into test animals it would not give them rabies, but it would protect them against the disease.

The question now facing Pasteur was — would the infected rabbit-cord extract have the same effect on humans? The opportunity to find out came unexpectedly in July, 1885. A nine-year-old boy, Joseph Meister,

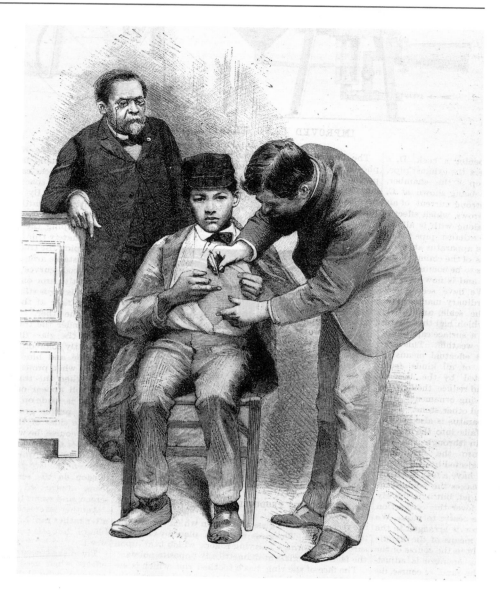

An American picture of Pasteur (left) **supervising the inoculation of a French shepherd boy who had been bitten by a rabid dog.**

had been bitten fourteen times by a rabid dog. He was not expected to live. Pasteur was placed in a terrible dilemma. He knew that his experimental vaccine offered at least the chance of a recovery. But he also knew that, if the vaccine failed, the boy might die. Pasteur might be charged with murder. He was not, after all, a qualified doctor, and his extraordinary success and self-confident manner had brought him

enemies as well as admirers. They would be glad to make trouble for him and ruin his reputation. Failure could mean that his brilliant career would end in controversy and personal disgrace. Despite the dangers, Pasteur decided to go ahead.

He began the treatment by injecting the boy with vaccine made from a fourteen-day-old rabbit cord. The next day he used a dose from a

thirteen-day-old cord. Each day the dose got stronger until finally he used a shot made from the spinal cord of a rabbit that had died only the day before. As Pasteur predicted, the previous injections had made the boy strong enough to resist the deadly infection. There was no reaction. He was safe. Pasteur had found an antidote to rabies.

The news of Pasteur's astonishing success spread across Europe in a

A dramatic painting of Pasteur taking saliva from a rabid dog.

matter of days. Still stunned by his own triumph, he found himself faced by a party of nineteen Russian peasants who had been bitten by a mad wolf two weeks earlier. It was a long time since they had been infected, and Pasteur feared that the disease had gone too far for him to save them. But he agreed to try — and sixteen survived.

Rabies

Rabies is an extremely dangerous and often deadly disease caused by a virus. As Pasteur correctly suspected, the virus was too small to be detected by the kind of microscope available to him at that time. Rabies affects mammals, especially dogs, wolves and foxes, and is transmitted to humans when saliva from an infected animal enters the bloodstream, usually as a result of a bite. The virus travels through the nervous system and attacks the brain, causing convulsions and muscle spasms. The patient alternates between calm and rage, and has difficulty swallowing food or drink. Even the sight of water can cause painful contractions of the throat (hydrophobia). The disease can develop in a few days or may take months to break out. It is usually fatal unless treatment is given quickly. Today, the vaccine therapy pioneered by Pasteur has been refined so that the disease can be treated effectively if caught at an early stage.

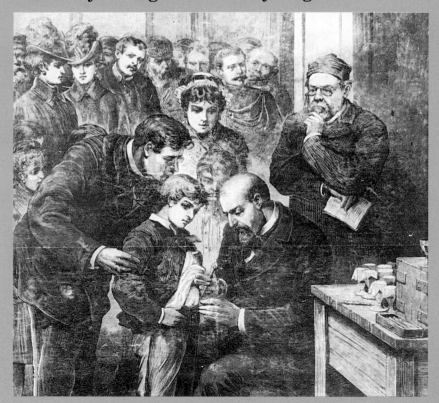

A crowd of distinguished visitors observe an inoculation against rabies. Even when proven successful, it was regarded as a risky procedure.

Tributes and Honors

Over the course of the next ten years, 20,000 victims of rabies were to be given the Pasteur treatment. Less than one in 200 died. Pasteur's breakthrough seized the imagination of the public. A movement began to collect funds for an Institute that would honor his work and help it continue. Contributions came from the Tsar of Russia, the Emperor of Brazil and the Turkish Sultan in Istanbul. In all, a sum of more than 2,000,000 francs was collected. The Pasteur Institute was dedicated in Paris on November 14, 1888, in the presence of the President of France. Pasteur himself was too overcome with emotion to deliver his own speech, which was read for him by his son:

"Two opposing laws seem to me to be now in contest. The one, a law of blood and death opening out each day new methods of destruction, forces nations to be always ready for battle. The other, a law of peace, work and health, whose only aim is to deliver man from the calamities which beset him ... Which of these two laws will prevail, God only knows. But of this we may be sure, science, in obeying the law of humanity, will always labor to enlarge the frontiers of life."

On December 27, 1892, an audience of hundreds of scientists and doctors gathered in Paris at the Sorbonne to pay tribute to Pasteur on his seventieth birthday. To emphasize the international

Inauguration of the Pasteur Institute, November 1888.

importance of his work, it was decided that the main address should be given by a foreigner, the British surgeon Joseph Lister. Lister began with the most handsome praise:

"I have the great honor of presenting to you the homage of Medicine and Surgery. Truly there does not exist in the whole world an individual to whom medical science owes more than you."

Lister himself certainly knew how Pasteur's discoveries:

"changed the treatment of wounds from an uncertain ... and too often disastrous business into a scientific and certainly beneficial art."

This alone would have merited the gratitude of the suffering and those who work to relieve their pain. But there was much more:

"Medicine owes not less than surgery ... You have raised the veil which for centuries has covered infectious diseases; you have discovered and demonstrated their microbic nature."

Lister (above) **salutes Pasteur at his 70th birthday tribute.** (Left) **Pasteur's magnificent tomb.**

Lister then laid special stress on the historic importance of Pasteur's success in overcoming rabies, although he was "neither a doctor nor a biologist."

Yet, even on this occasion, when the leaders of the medical world were united in their praise, Lister, as their appointed spokesman had to admit, at least indirectly, that there were still "a few ignoramuses" who did not "recognize the grandeur of your achievements."

Pasteur replied, through his son, that in the long run he was confident that:

" ... the future will belong not to the conquerors but to the saviors of mankind."

If anyone deserves to be numbered among the saviors, it is surely Pasteur himself.

Seven years later, Pasteur's health finally gave way. On September 28, 1895, he died. His dying words were:

"One must work; one must work. I have done what I could."

The tanner's son was given a State funeral and buried in a magnificent tomb in the crypt at the Pasteur Institute. The walls of the crypt were decorated with paintings of chickens, lambs, dogs and children whose lives had been saved by Pasteur's work.

The Pasteur Institute

Apart from conducting scientific research, the Pasteur Institute in Paris trains researchers, manufactures vaccines and sends its experts to fight disease throughout the world. In the few years in which he was the active director of the Institute, Pasteur sent Albert Calmette to Saigon to organize a vaccination campaign against smallpox. He also sent Alexandre Yersin to Hong Kong to battle with bubonic plague.

Pasteur did not live long enough to see Yersin identify the **bacillus** that causes bubonic plague and develop a **serum** that would protect people against it. But he did see the Institute's first great triumph, Pierre Roux's cure for diphtheria, then a disease deadly to small children.

Since Pasteur's day, the Institute named in his honor has developed the BCG vaccine, which prevents tuberculosis, and a typhus vaccine, which weakened the power of another age-old killer that had earlier killed two of Pasteur's own children. In West Africa, mobile vaccination teams helped stamp out yellow fever.

The Pasteur Institute began its life as an ambitious enterprise, but even its founder might be astonished to see how it has grown in a century, with 2,000 people employed at its headquarters today, and as many more working in nearly 100 field stations around the world.

(Left) **The original Pasteur Institute as it looks today.** (Right) **The work goes on. Emile Roux of the Institute tries to find a diphtheria vaccine (1895).**

Joseph Meister

Joseph Meister (1876–1940) was the nine-year-old boy Pasteur saved from a horrible death from rabies. When he grew up he became a gatekeeper at the Pasteur Institute. In 1940, long after Pasteur's death, Meister was still serving faithfully as the Institute's gatekeeper. France had once again been invaded by Germany and a Nazi officer came to the Institute, demanding to see inside Pasteur's tomb. The devoted old man refused. When the Nazi insisted, Meister killed himself rather than desecrate the grave of his savior. Today, a statue of a small boy stands on the lawn outside the Institute — the boy is Joseph Meister.

A statue to the memory of Joseph Meister stands outside the Institute where Pasteur is buried.

Find Out More ...

Important Books

Louis Pasteur by Rae Bains (Troll, 1985)

Pasteur and Modern Science (rev. ed.) by Rene J. Dubos (Science Tech Publishers, 1988)

Fighting Hero of Science by Madeleine P. Grant and Louis P. Grant (McGraw-Hill, 1959)

Louis Pasteur: The Scientist Who Found the Cause of Infectious Disease and Invented Pasteurization by Beverley Rich (Gareth Stevens Inc. 1989)

The Pasteurization of France by Latour Bruno (Harvard University Press, 1988)

Louis Pasteur: Young Scientist by Francene Sabin (Troll, 1983)

Important Dates

1822	December 22, born at Dôle, France
1829-31	Studies at primary school in Arbois
1831-39	Studies at the College d'Arbois
1839-42	Studies at College Royal de Besançon
1842-43	Studies at Barbet's School and Lycée St. Louis, Paris
1843-48	Studies chemistry at École Normale Supérieure
1847-57	Experiments in crystallography
1849	Lecturer at Strasbourg Marries Marie Laurent
1854	Dean of The Faculty of Science, Lille University
1857	Director of Scientific Studies at École Normale, Paris
1857-65	Studies fermentation problems
1863-67	Teaches at École des Beaux-Arts, Paris
1865-70	Investigates silkworm disease
1867-74	Professor of Chemistry at the Sorbonne
1868	Commander of the Legion of Honor; suffers a stroke
1870-71	Franco-Prussian war; returns honorary degree to University of Bonn
1871-76	Studies problems of beer-making
1875	Stands unsuccessfully for election to the French Senate
1881	Elected to French Academy
1882	Demonstrates effectiveness of anthrax vaccine
1883	Awarded an annuity of 25,000 francs by French government
1885	Vaccinates Joseph Meister, a victim of rabies
1887	Suffers second stroke
1888	Becomes Director of Pasteur Institute
1892	Receives Lister's tribute at Sorbonne
1895	September 28, dies

Glossary

Anesthetics Drugs that make people unconscious and so unable to feel pain.

Antiseptics Chemicals that kill bacteria.

Bacillus A kind of bacteria that causes disease.

Beet Root vegetable, also called beetroot.

Crystallography The study of crystals, their structures and properties.

Fermentation The slow chemical breakdown of a substance, begun by microorganisms such as yeast, bacteria, etc.

Germs A popular name for microorganisms, particularly those that cause disease.

Immune Unable to catch a certain disease because the body is already defended against it.

Immunization Making people immune by giving them a mild dose of a disease.

Inoculation Another word for immunization.

Lycée A French secondary school.

Microorganisms Tiny life-forms that can be seen only through a microscope.

Pasteurization Sterilization of food and drink, especially milk, by Pasteur's method of heating it to kill off any bacteria.

Prussia Old European state that is now part of East Germany.

Serum Liquid made from the blood of an animal that is immune to a particular disease. The liquid is then injected into other animals or people so that they also become immune to that disease.

Sorbonne An ancient college in Paris, forming part of the University.

Stereochemistry An area of chemistry that studies the arrangement of atoms in chemical substances.

Vaccines Substances used to immunize people or animals, making them immune to particular diseases.

Index

Picture Acknowledgements

The publishers would like to thank the following for their kind permission to reproduce their photographs in this book: Ann Ronan Picture Library, 8,9 (bottom), 10,12,17,18,20,27,30; Institut Pasteur, 4,7,9 (top), 11,21,22,23,24,25,26,29; Mansell Collection, cover; Mary Evans, frontispiece,5,13,14,15,16; Popperfoto,6,28.